Business Plans
in a week

IAIN MAITLAND

Hodder & Stoughton

A MEMBER OF THE HODDER HEADLINE GROUP

Orders: please contact Bookpoint Ltd, 130 Milton Park, Abingdon, Oxon
OX14 4SB.
Telephone: (44) 01235 827720, Fax: (44) 01235 400454. Lines are open from
9.00–6.00, Monday to Saturday, with a 24 hour message answering service.
Email address: orders@bookpoint.co.uk

British Library Cataloguing in Publication Data
A catalogue record for this title is available from the British Library

ISBN 0 340 849630

First published 1996
Impression number   10 9 8 7 6 5 4 3 2 1
Year   2007 2006 2005 2004 2003 2002

Typeset by SX Composing DTP, Rayleigh, Essex.
Printed in Great Britain for Hodder & Stoughton Educational, a division of
Hodder Headline Plc, 338 Euston Road, London NW1 3BH by Cox and
Wyman Ltd., Reading, Berkshire.

chartered
management
institute

inspiring leaders

The leading organisation for professional management

As the champion of management, the Chartered Management Institute shapes and supports the managers of tomorrow. By sharing intelligent insights and setting standards in management development, the Institute helps to deliver results in a dynamic world.

Setting and raising standards

The Institute is a nationally accredited organisation, responsible for setting standards in management and recognising excellence through the award of professional qualifications.

Encouraging development, improving performance

The Institute has a vast range of development programmes, qualifications, information resources and career guidance to help managers and their organisations meet new challenges in a fast-changing environment.

Shaping opinion

With in-depth research and regular policy surveys of its 91,000 individual members and 520 corporate members, the Chartered Management Institute has a deep understanding of the key issues. Its view is informed, intelligent and respected.

For more information call 01536 204222 or visit www.managers.org.uk

C O N T E N T S

■ I N T R O D U C T I O N ■

All businesses should plan ahead, especially when they wish to raise finance, attract investment, encourage assistance or improve their overall performance. They need to know exactly *what* they want, and *when* and *how* they are going to get there – otherwise, they cannot expect to progress, let alone achieve their objectives.

A business plan can help them to do this. It is a document which sets out the activities of a firm and explains how and when its various objectives will be reached. Usually, such a plan consists of a commercial section detailing key aspects of the concern, a financial section outlining money matters, and appendices which substantiate and elaborate on these two sections. In essence, a business plan provides a framework for the firm to work *within* and *towards*.

The aim of this book is to cut through all the theory and waffle that exists about business plans and show you how to write a successful one. We shall look at this core skill on a clear, step-by-step basis, taking one step each day as follows:

Sunday	Understanding business plans
Monday	Making preparatory notes
Tuesday	Composing the commercial section
Wednesday	Compiling the financial section
Thursday	Adding the appendices
Friday	Submitting a business plan
Saturday	Presenting a business plan

Understanding business plans

Today, we will take a broad, introductory look at business plans. We need to understand what makes them successful before we can go on to write one over the rest of the week. In particular, we should consider their:

- contents
- uses
- key features

Contents

Not surprisingly, all business plans are different, but most of them will contain three main sections:

- a commercial section
- a financial section
- appendices

A commercial section
In this first section, we would normally include some preliminary materials such as a title page, contents page and introduction. These would then be followed by text about our business, products and services, team, market and overall objectives. The names and order of these subjects and the precise information given about them may vary from one plan to another, but they should all be covered in some detail somewhere in this section.

A financial section
Equally important, if not more so in some instances, the financial section of a business plan will usually incorporate a profit budget and cash-flow forecast indicating the estimated profits and ongoing cash position within the firm over a given period of time. These will often be accompanied by past or projected – or both – annual accounts, such as a profit and loss account and a balance sheet, plus details of current financial circumstances and requirements.

Appendices
This final section comprises photographs, samples, letters, forms, documents and other items of independent origin

which verify and occasionally add to all of the statements, financial facts and figures laid down in the commercial and financial sections. In many respects, these appendices can be viewed as the foundation of a successful business plan: without them, the preceding text is simply a mass of unsubstantiated opinions and hearsay.

Here is a checklist of what we might include in our business plan:

1 Commercial section:

- title page
- contents page
- introduction
- the business
- products and services
- the team
- the market
- objectives

2 Financial section:

- profit budget
- cash-flow forecast
- past accounts
- future accounts
- current financial circumstances
- financial requirements

3 Appendices:

- photographs
- samples
- letters
- forms
- documents
- other items

Uses

We may compile a business plan for various reasons. Most often, it will be used to:

- raise finance
- attract investment
- encourage assistance
- improve performance

Raise finance
If we need funds to start, buy or expand a firm in some way, a plan may be sent to a prospective lender such as a bank or building society manager, charitable trust, venture capital house or even family or friends who have savings or redundancy money available. Hopefully, we can convince the relevant parties both that we have a viable proposal and that we will be able to make capital and interest payments on time.

Attract investment
Similarly, the business plan could be used to attract investment, and would in this case be written to highlight the firm's forthcoming activities and potential profits, and

the possible risks and returns for would-be investors. Such a plan may be forwarded to wealthy individuals and to organisations like venture capital institutions which specialise in investing in up-and-coming companies, especially those trading in new and innovative activities.

Encourage assistance
Sometimes, we need help from other people and organisations in order to trade successfully and prosper. Perhaps we want a prospective landlord to grant a lease to us, a supplier to enter into a sole agency agreement for our town, or a fellow trader to allow us to use their storage and distribution facilities. These parties may be more willing to do what we want if they have been given a plan which outlines both our requirements and intentions and the mutual benefits arising from them.

Improve performance
Even if we do not require external finance, investment or assistance, it is still a good idea to draw up a business plan anyway, for our own internal use. Preparing commercial and financial sections (and appendices where appropriate) enables us to assess our business in an objective manner. We may get to know it better, along with its individual strengths and weaknesses, and be able to set more realistic objectives as a consequence of this increased knowledge and understanding.

Just as significantly, a business plan provides us with a commercial and financial framework against which we can regularly compare our performance to see if we are on course to achieve our objectives. Possible problems such as rising costs and imminent cash shortfalls can hopefully be spotted and resolved well in advance. If reviewed and

amended at monthly intervals, our plan enables us to
monitor, control and improve the overall performance of
our business – perhaps this is the most important function
of a business plan.

Key features

So, we know what a business plan is, what it contains and
how we can use it. We now need to think about those key
features that distinguish a successful business plan from an
unsuccessful one. Obviously, we will wish to incorporate
these into the plan that we are going to write.

Ideally, our business plan will be:

- well researched
- adapted
- attractive
- understandable
- realistic
- well supported

Well researched

A successful business plan is researched fully, and is only completed once all the commercial, financial and supporting information that may need to be included in it has been gathered together. The plan should create the impression that the writer knows everything there is to know and can prove it. As soon as the reader thinks of something they wish to see, they should be able to find it. And if they want proof of a statement, it should be readily available in he appendices.

Adapted

Of course, not all of the facts and figures that we are going to collect should be put into the plan – otherwise it might run to tens or even hundreds of pages! Its content, structure, emphasis and length must vary according to what our particular reader wants to know about and how much time they have to read it. For example, a bank manager wishes to know about commercial activities but only in relation to likely profits, cash flow and financial requirements. A prospective landlord, on the other hand, may want to learn about how our business and activities might affect other tenants, but little else. However much information we want to incorporate – and there is no right or wrong length for a business plan – we must try to keep it as brief and to the point as we can. Always asking 'Is this relevant?' before noting anything down should help us to achieve this. The reader will only have a certain amount of time to study our plan, and needs to be able to do it swiftly. We can assist them in doing this by omitting irrelevant, superfluous and repetitive material.

Attractive
A winning business plan must have a smart and professional appearance, especially if it is being sent out to raise finance, attract investment or encourage assistance in some way. This will give the writer an efficient, businesslike image and should put the reader in a more

favourable mood towards both them and any proposition that they are making. Clearly, the business proposal itself must still be a viable one if it is to be accepted, but it obviously helps to get the reader on our side as far as possible.

Our business plan must be put inside a clean and classy file or folder: this not only creates a professional impression but also protects the material from becoming torn and dirty as it is being passed around. We should choose a file which matches our image – colourful and jazzy if we are artistic, plain and dark if we are methodical and serious. For easy identification, it is a good idea to place a white sticker on the front of the file and type (or write neatly) the title of the plan on it along with our name, address, 'phone/fax number, e-mail address and/or web site and the date. A business logo adds a classy touch too:

KALEIDOSCOPE
A
BUSINESS PROPOSAL
BY
TOM HUDSON
2, THE COTTAGES, NEWTOWN, SUFFOLK FE7 3BH
TEL/FAX: 01394 770512
E-MAIL: THUDSON@NVC.COM
DATE: 1 MAY 2002

To emphasise our professionalism, we need to use top-quality, A4 paper, perhaps selecting white or another shade if we want to coordinate colours to achieve a particular style and image. The text should be typed, rather than handwritten and amateurish, and should be set out carefully. We ought to include generous margins at the top, sides and bottom of each page, plenty of headings and subheadings, short paragraphs of similar length, and bullet points where appropriate. These all help to improve the overall appearance, making it easier to read, and give the reader sufficient room in which to note comments and queries.

Here is an example of what we should be aiming for:

About Kaleidoscope

- *Its purpose*
  Kaleidoscope is being set up in order to meet the needs of those families who wish to hire rather than buy nursery goods and equipment, typically overnight and on an occasional basis
- *Its location*
  It will be based in a newly built, 500-square-metre showroom alongside of our home. This is within two minutes' walking distance of the town's only health centre, St John's Playgroup and Newtown Primary School (see 'Appendix 2: Newtown Map' on pages 3–4 of the appendices)
- *Its products and services*
  Initially, we will stock the following goods:
  - moses baskets
  - carrycots
  - cribs
  - baby bouncers
  - baby walkers
  - highchairs

We should always submit clean copies of typed sheets, rather than photocopies which would create the impression that this is little more than a circular being sent out to everyone. (We can, however, put extra, clean copies of the plan at the back of our file or folder if we know that several people will wish to study it.) The text must be free from any spelling mistakes, typing errors or inaccuracies such as incorrectly added figures. These will confuse and muddle the reader and damage our reputation. We need to check, check and check again – and then retype, if necessary.

Understandable

Our language must match the reader's knowledge and understanding of the subject matter. We should use clear, simple words and phrases when addressing a layperson who may be bewildered by trade jargon. Likewise, we should incorporate technical expressions where appropriate when writing to an expert who might otherwise feel patronised. The key to success here is to think carefully about what our reader knows, and to pitch our language at the right level. It is important that we never automatically assume they are as familiar with the subject as we are – this is rarely the case.

Whatever we have to say, we must ensure that we use specific words and phrases, rather than vague ones such as 'good', 'nice', 'better than' and 'cheaper than' which will be defined differently by each reader. For example, '£33.95' is understood clearly, whereas 'a good price' means nothing. Humorous comments and statements must be avoided at all times too. What we find funny may be interpreted in another way by a person with an alternative sense of humour. Our joke could be seen as flippant and, when finance or investment is being sought, humour is often considered to be inappropriate.

Realistic

Obviously, we need to sound 100 per cent confident and enthusiastic about our firm and its prospects – after all, if we are not, we cannot expect the reader to be either! Nevertheless, we must not get too carried away, as this may make us sound foolish and could undermine what we are stating. Most readers will possess some knowledge of what we are writing about, and will be able to distinguish between facts and fantasy.

Our statements and financial figures need to be sensible and achievable. We should base them on solid, reliable evidence such as past income and expenditure and definite sales orders. Prospective difficulties must be addressed fully rather than being glossed over or ignored completely. We should identify and then explain clearly how we are going to overcome, or at least cope with, them. By not referring to them, we simply appear evasive or incompetent. It is sensible to deal in detail only with the immediate future, namely the coming year: the longer ahead we look, the more speculative our comments become. Our reader is more interested in reality than hopes and dreams.

Well supported

A successful business plan always backs up its commercial and financial sections with independent evidence in its appendices. Our comments alone will not be accepted at face value, especially if large sums of money are involved. We therefore have to be willing and able to prove everything we say is true by supplying additional, verifying material from reputable sources, and ideally, independent ones.

Summary

To sum up what we have learned today:

- A business plan usually contains:
  - a commercial section
  - a financial section
  - appendices

- It can be used to:
  - raise finance
  - attract investment
  - encourage assistance
  - improve performance

- A successful business plan is:
  - well researched
  - adapted
  - attractive
  - understandable
  - realistic
  - supported

Making preparatory notes

Following Sunday's work, we know what we are aiming for. The next step is to draw up some detailed, preparatory notes for our own successful business plan. This means:

- conducting internal research
- using external sources
- accumulating appropriate information

Conducting internal research

Much of the information we need to put into our business plan can be obtained relatively easily, from in-house sources:

- our own knowledge
- our colleagues
- books and records

Our own knowledge

More often than not, our understanding of the business will be greater than anyone else's. We may have established the firm and perhaps now sell the goods, recruit the team, deal personally with customers, and so on. Who else knows as much as us? Probably nobody! We should therefore draw upon our own background knowledge and information before proceeding further.

Possibly the best way of doing this is to ask ourselves lots of questions to see if we can answer them. Here are some to start us off:

- What is our business?
- What does it do?
- Whereabouts is it located?
- What are the premises like?
- What equipment, machinery and vehicles do we have?
- What do we sell?
- What are our products and services like?
- What are our rivals' goods and services like?
- Who works for the firm?
- What are their backgrounds?
- What do they do?
- What are their strengths and weaknesses?
- Who are our customers?
- How much do we know about them?
- Who are our competitors?
- What do we know about them?
- What is the marketplace like?
- How much do we know about it?
- What are our personal goals?
- What are our business objectives?
- How have we been doing financially?
- What are our finances like now?
- What will our finances be like in the future?
- What cash will be available?
- What profits will we make in the future?
- How can we prove all this information?

Our colleagues
In a larger business with various departments for
purchasing, production, marketing, administration,
personnel and so forth, some of the data required for the
plan may have to be obtained by approaching our work

colleagues. Whoever we talk to, we do need to be able to distinguish between opinions and facts. Generally, facts are better than opinions, unless the latter come from independent, reputable sources – which our colleagues are not!

Books and records
Whatever the size of our firm, the books and records that we have accumulated so far will be invaluable to us when we are composing our business plan. In particular, we will find it helpful to refer to previous annual accounts, purchase agreements, sales records and orders, and the like. Details can be taken from these and discussed in the text of the plan, with key documents being placed in the appendices for verification.

Normally, most of the facts that we need for the commercial and financial sections of our business plan will be available in-house. However, we need to remember that everything we write about has to be proved, and this means obtaining supporting data from outside the firm. Our word alone is not enough: other people's carry more weight.

Using external sources

There are many external sources of information and advice available to us. We should consider all of them, and then approach those which are most likely to be of assistance. The following are usually worth contacting:

- banks/building societies
- customers
- suppliers
- competitors
- accountants
- solicitors
- agents
- associations
- government
- media
- Internet

Banks/building societies
As our bank manager is probably going to receive our plan, it is sensible to get in touch with them beforehand to find out exactly what they want from us. The majority of banks and building societies provide ready-made business plan, profit budget and cash-flow forecast forms for us to complete, and can supply guidance on how to fill these in correctly. Pamphlets and booklets on general business issues and specific details on financial matters are available too. These all make useful background reading.

Customers
Those people and firms who buy our goods and services are an excellent source of advice. They can tell us all we need to know – and to write – about them, including their location, characteristics, wants and needs. In addition, they can give us opinions about our concern and our goods and services which may be useful additions to our appendices. Their comments about our rivals might be revealing as well.

Suppliers
Our suppliers will obviously be able to provide facts and figures about the raw materials, component parts and stocks that we are purchasing from them, along with further, helpful information about mutual customers,

competitors and the marketplace. Although some of their additional comments may be biased, these will usually contain one or two points of use to us.

Competitors
Many small businesses compete amicably against each other, with the overall aim of surviving against larger companies trading nearby. If we can establish friendly relationships, we may be able to draw on their knowledge of goods, services, customers and the market. Clearly, we may find out more about *them* as well, which will enable us to then write about them with greater accuracy.

Accountants
Costly though they are, an accountant can put us in touch with potential financiers, provide advice on all money matters, help us to write our financial section, and give our business plan a greater veneer of respectability. It is usually wise to choose an accountant on the basis of recommendations from fellow traders we can trust. We need to be aware of the likely costs involved in using them, and evaluate these alongside of the possible benefits.

Solicitors
We could approach a solicitor for guidance on legal issues that we need to refer to in our plan – partnership agreements, contracts of sale, freehold deeds, leasehold agreements and planning permission, amongst other items. As with an accountant, we should make our choice from personal recommendations and compare the expense against the advantages of referring to them. Evidently, they are invaluable in some instances.

Agents
Business transfer agents who specialise in selling going
concerns will be able to supply data about businesses for
sale, what to look for and how to value them, as well as
information about freehold and leasehold properties, and
how to agree rents – all potential text or appendices
material for us. Similarly, estate agents can comment on
freehold and leasehold premises, prices, rents and rates in
our region which may be of some value to our business
plan.

Associations
Local chambers of commerce or trade run by business
people in the community can be a good source of off-the-
record advice about what is happening in the area.
Representative associations in our trade or industry can
provide or verify much of the commercial information
needed. Membership of a nationwide, small-business
association confers many benefits for members, including
an advisory service on most business issues.

Government
Our local council can be a helpful source of information on
such subjects as low-cost finance and grants available,
planning-permission procedures and forthcoming
developments. Some councils even employ small-business
advisers who can assist in the writing of business plans. A
variety of statistics, surveys and reports are continually
being produced by national government and supplied
through its departments such as the Department of Trade
and Industry. Many of these contain useful background
details for our plan.

Media

Newspapers, magazines and web sites may have included
articles about our business, products, services, employees,
customers and competitors at some time in the past. We
may find it beneficial to refer to these once more when
compiling our commercial section in particular. Copies of
recent articles could then be placed within the appendices
to support any comments made. Don't forget to search for
information on-line, perhaps via www.google.com.

Here are some other sources of potential use to us:

- architects
- surveyors
- illustrators
- photographers
- printers
- insurance brokers
- libraries
- market research companies

Accumulating appropriate information

We now need to start sorting through the mass of
information that has come to us from all the different
sources, making notes which subsequently can form the
basis of our business plan. We could use these headings:

- The business
- Products and services
- The team
- The market
- Objectives
- Finance
- Appendices

The business
Under this heading, we could jot down notes about our
firm or business idea, including whatever we think is most
relevant in our situation. Typically, we might write about its
history, activities and current position, location and
premises, equipment, machinery and vehicles. It is up to us
to decide what our reader wants to see.

Products and services
Here, we might note down information about the numbers
and types of products and services that we offer, along with
their main features and selling points. It is important to
make notes too about rival goods and services, comparing
and contrasting these with our own. We need to be
especially realistic at this point, being aware of our
shortcomings and how we are going to deal with them.

The team
Beneath this heading, we should focus on ourselves as well
as our colleagues and employees, as appropriate. In
particular, we should note our individual careers to date,

skills, knowledge, experiences, strengths and weaknesses, and how we all fit together to form a good team.

The market
Here, we should concentrate on our customers – their numbers, types, locations and purchasing habits. We need to make notes about our competitors too – numbers, types, locations, activities, strengths and weaknesses. We could also take a broader look at the marketplace itself, especially its size, changes and developments taking place, and future prospects.

Objectives
It is a good idea for us to write out our personal and business objectives for the short, medium and long term – for the next year, three years and thereafter. We must be cautious, though: a lender will want to see that we are not being overoptimistic and therefore unrealistic.

Finance

If we are planning to include a financial section for a bank manager, or whomever, we should sketch out some preliminary notes about our finances to date, likely future sales, costs and profits, and possible forthcoming cash-flow into and out of our account, as well as our current financial circumstances and requirements. If we are trying to raise finance, these notes are essential – indeed, as important as all of the other notes put together.

Appendices

Below this final heading, we should make a note of those items which we can put in to back up our statements. Here is a list of what we might decide to include:

- press cuttings
- map
- property particulars
- photographs of equipment
- product samples
- suppliers' price lists
- our price lists
- sales literature
- competitors' price lists
- competitors' sales literature
- curricula vitae
- certificates/diplomas
- partnership-agreement documents
- company-formation documents
- sales records
- sales orders
- quotes/estimates of costs
- annual accounts
- proof of security
- accountant's/solicitor's comments

Of course, this does not mean we have to include all of these items – we should consider them all carefully, and then select the relevant ones.

Summary

During Monday, we have carried out the following, important tasks:

- conducted internal research, drawing on our own knowledge, and referring to colleagues, books and records too
- used external sources to verify and enhance the information we have gathered together
- accumulated appropriate information about the business, products and services, team, market, objectives and finance, as well as appropriate information for the appendices

Composing the commercial section

Having completed our preparatory work, we can now move on to make a start on the plan itself – by writing that all-important commercial section. Today, therefore, we will consider:

- the preliminaries
- our business
- the products and services
- our team
- the market
- our objectives

The preliminaries

The commercial section should begin with:

> * a title page
> * a contents page
> * an introduction

A title page
This should simply repeat the information given on the file
or folder in which the business plan is being submitted.
Restating its title plus our name, address, telephone/fax
number, e-mail address and/or web site and the date of
compilation will ensure that the plan is instantly
recognisable if it is separated from its file.

A contents page
Whoever is studying our business plan will wish to be able
to find relevant topics promptly. Thus, a precise and
accurate list of contents must be included showing the
order of the various subjects we have dealt with and the
respective pages to be referred to. We need to draft the
contents page and number all of the pages *after* we have
completed the entire plan. If we do it any earlier, we will
then inevitably think of two or three other items which
need to be put somewhere in the text. Renumbered pages –
with '11a' and '11b' slotted in and '12' rewritten as '13' and
so on – look sloppy and convey a slapdash image. We must
avoid this at all costs.

An introduction
We should never underestimate the significance of an

introduction: it can mean the difference between success and failure. Bankers, prospective investors and other interested parties will probably be busy, with little time to study every business plan sent to them. Their initial impression of our plan therefore will decide whether it receives either their full, undivided attention or no more than a cursory glance before rejection.

To convince the recipient that our plan deserves to be studied, we should broadly summarise the text. We might say what our business is selling, who our customers are and what objectives we have. Most important of all to the reader, we must then explain *what it is* that we want them to do for us – provide finance, supply goods or whatever. Ideally, we will also point out *what is in it for them* if they do help us – after all, *that*, more than anything else, is going to persuade them to read on!

As with the contents page, we should write the introduction once we have finished the rest of the plan – otherwise we will only have to redo it if we subsequently decide to change the order of the subjects. Looking at each section in turn, 'Our business', 'Products and services' and so forth, we should sum them up in one or two sentences. If these are all then put together and trimmed to remove vague and repetitive comments, we should have a first-rate introduction which is both brief *and* informative.

Our business

With our earlier notes to hand, we can start writing about the business, in particular:

- its background
- its location
- its premises

Its background

If the business has been trading for some time, we should set out its track record to date – when, where and why it was launched, how it has progressed to reach its current position, its achievements and the obstacles overcome. If we are buying a business, we should say why it is for sale – and the reason should be the *real* one, which may not necessarily be the same as that given by the vendor! On the other hand, we could be getting ready to start a business from scratch. If so, we must supply background information about our ideas instead – what made us think of this business, why we believe it will be successful, how, where and when we will start trading. Everything we write down should be supported by substantiating evidence – balance sheets, profit and loss accounts, a business transfer agent's details, an accountant's letter, newspaper and magazine clippings and the like.

Its location

We should write about the location too – the reasons for basing the business there, its advantages, and its disadvantages and how we are working to overcome them. We must also mention any anticipated changes taking place in the locality, such as a new factory or road, and state how we will deal with the opportunities and challenges that arise as a result.

An excellent way of supporting this text is to slot a map into the appendices. On this, we should highlight the locations of our business, suppliers, customers, competitors and other key data such as influential neighbours and any attractions which draw people into the area, like free car parks. Sometimes, it can be helpful to include two maps, one a close-up of the firm and its immediate vicinity, the other a map of the town or trading region.

Its premises
If we are buying a property, we should note the asking price, the amount of capital we have to invest, why we want to buy instead of rent and what we will do if the business fails. We must be realistic here. If we are renting, we should refer to any premium we will have to pay, the amount and frequency of rental payments, service charges and the date of the next rent review. Again, we must say what we will do with the lease if the business is unsuccessful.

Next, we should specify the dimensions of our premises and the internal and external layouts, plus the equipment, machinery and vehicles used. We need to explain whether these are owned or leased, how long they will last for, when we will need to replace them and what they *are* and *will be* worth.

Again, it is essential that we substantiate everything we have stated to prove it is all true. We might think about putting in the estate agent's particulars, a copy of the freehold deeds or leasehold agreement, the solicitor's and surveyor's reports, and photographs and diagrams of equipment, machinery and vehicles, as appropriate.

The products and services

Going on with this section, we should concentrate on detailing our products and services as appropriate – more specifically:

- their main features
- their unique selling points

Their main features
We must state what our products and services are and how they contribute towards our stock and sales levels. We should outline what these products look like, how they work and what they can be used for. With services, we must state what they involve us doing for customers. It may be a good idea to explain how we make or buy our goods – production processes, output and quality control, suppliers, terms and conditions of sale.

We should also mention our prices plus any discounts offered for bulk buys or prompt payments, saying why goods and services are priced at that level, and showing them to be competitively priced *and* profitable. It is important to write about advertising and selling methods too – how we advertise and sell our products and services, why our choices are effective, who sells our goods, how they are distributed, and so on.

We then have to decide what verifying documents should be included in the appendices. It is useful to put in photographs, illustrations and newspaper cuttings – even samples of our goods, if there is room for them. As relevant, we could also include production schedules, suppliers' price lists, letters or invoices stating costs, our price guide and advertising and promotional materials.

Their unique selling points
If our products and services are to sell, they must have some obvious advantages over competing goods. Thus, we should provide a short list of our main rivals, with brief descriptions of each of them. We need to put the same type of information about our rivals into the appendices as we did for our own products and services – photos, price lists and sales and advertising literature are a must. Adding samples is a sound idea as well.

It is important to highlight the advantages that our goods have over competing ones *and* how these will be maintained. Being realistic, we must also refer to any disadvantages that our products and services may have, explaining how we intend to remedy them. A timetable showing when the changes and improvements will be made may be a useful addition to the business plan.

Our team

When composing the commercial section, we must never forget to detail the most important ingredient of any business: the people within it – that means us! Therefore, we should make sure that we include one or two paragraphs about:

- ourselves
- colleagues and employees

Ourselves

It is often said that most financiers and investors are primarily backing the *people* involved, with money and assistance being provided on the strength of their personalities, skills, knowledge, experiences and finances. Every statement we make about ourselves must indicate that we have what it takes to be successful!

It is probably best to approach this part of the text in a chronological order, working forward from our school or college days through our career or business history up to the present time. We need to verify our comments with a curriculum vitae, photocopies of certificates and diplomas, press cuttings and even congratulatory letters about our work from former employers or satisfied customers. Let's not hide our light under a bushel!

Colleagues and employees

We should describe our business colleagues in the same way that we wrote about ourselves, outlining their careers to date, drawing in personalities, skills and so forth, and saying what they'll be doing for the firm. If we are jointly controlling a business, it is sensible to discuss the key points of our partnership agreement, how much capital is being introduced by each person, the salaries to be paid, how profits and losses will be shared out, the length of the partnership and how it can be dissolved.

We can then refer to our key employees, such as managers, detailing their past and present jobs plus future roles in the business. After this, we could list the remaining employees, perhaps by name, job title and duties. If there are many of them, it is wiser to state the numbers employed in each department instead. We must not forget to mention the wages we pay to them, either per employee or per department. If we have to buy in any services that cannot be done in-house, we should refer to these here as well, along with a note of the expenses involved.

Relevant documents for our appendices would include curricula vitae of key personnel, copies of certificates and diplomas, partnership agreements and company-formation documents plus written estimates of likely professional fees – in short, anything that will back up what we have just put down in writing.

The market

Ever conscious of our preparatory notes, we can press ahead and write about the marketplace, and most notably:

- the customers
- the competitors

The customers
If there are not too many of them, we should supply key customers' names and addresses here *or* in the appendices, as appropriate. Alternatively, we can identify them in terms of sex, age, income and occupation (or a combination of these). It is sensible to say how many there are, where they are located and how much, and when and why, they will buy from us. We can then discuss the market as a whole plus our share of this. It is advisable to explain how these circumstances may change in the future, and how we will deal with these developments.

We should substantiate the comments we have made about

our customers by incorporating documents such as sales records, orders and a map showing where they are. It is wise to support our statements about the market by obtaining matching assessments from reliable, independent sources: chambers of commerce, trade associations and the like.

The competitors
We ought to supply a thumbnail sketch of each competitor in terms of their history, activities, location, premises, goods, customers and market share. Being realistic, we need to say how they are better than us and how we intend to cancel out these advantages. Also, we should state how they are less successful than we are and what we are going to do to keep ahead of them.

As always, we have to back our comments with hard evidence. We should slip into the appendices a web site address if appropriate, any newspaper cuttings about their recent activities, successes and failures, a map showing where they are based, photographs of their premises, and sales literature too. We must prove that what we have stated is a true and fair assessment and not just our personal, biased opinion.

Our objectives

The recipient now has all the key commercial details. However we still have some important information to put across and it can make the difference between our success or failure. We need to set out our objectives; our plans and intentions for the next year, three years and beyond. The key to success is to be realistic. All of the good work done so far will be undone if we get too carried away. We conclude this commercial section – and today's work – by setting out our objectives. We can divide these as follows:

- The short term,
- The medium term
- The long term

The short term
The short term covers the next year; it is the immediate future. These goals are easy to set out as we have already talked about them in the commercial section. Read back over what has been written so far. It is a good idea to write them down so that we can prioritise them in their order of importance to us. It is essential that these are all achievable. Too many entrepreneurs seek to impress by 'talking big', deliberately exaggerating what they expect to achieve in order to impress. But most bank managers, for example, have heard it all before. They are more interested in realistic plans than empty pipedreams.

The recipient will be interested in facts. So we should take each of our goals and show how it will be achieved. If we say we are aiming for a certain turnover, we should refer to our financial forms to show how we will build up to this. Whenever we write anything, we must always think how we can back it up. A comment or assurance that is not supported in any way is not worth making. Anyone can say, 'I'll have the biggest business in town next year' but it is meaningless unless it is supported by hard facts and figures.

The medium term
This period of time covers the two years after the first year – the second and third year in business. It is an often overlooked fact that most businesses fail in the first three years, and most of those in the first year itself. In light of this, we should be toning down any thoughts we might have about world domination! It is sensible to have sewn the seeds of later success in our short term goals. In the medium term, we should be looking to build cautiously on these. What many entrepreneurs do wrong is to leap from 'starting up' to, say, 'owning a chain of shops' in the medium term. But a lot needs to happen in-between for this to be realised. Taking a shop as an example, we should be thinking about learning 'what's what' in that first year. In the medium term, we should be thinking about testing new lines, with a view to opening a second shop in due course. But only when we are ready to do so.

The long term
The long term begins in three years – and goes on indefinitely! It is sensible here to sketch out our overall goals – to have several shops, for example. But we need to couch these in realistic and cautious terms. In business,

three years is a long time and most recipients will know that all sorts of things can happen in that time. They will want to see where we are going in general terms, but will not expect us to back it up with facts and figures as it is too far away. We should keep these goals in proportion to what is happening now. If we are seeking funds to start a shop, having one or two other shops nearby sounds realistic. A shop in every town all over the world is not!

If the reader isn't interested in seeing a financial section – perhaps a would-be landlord just wants to check that our commercial activities won't clash with those of our fellow tenants – then we will conclude the text here. Being concise, we could possibly remind the recipient what it is we want from them, and how this will both help us to reach our objectives and benefit them as well.

Summary

Today, we have discussed what goes into the commercial section of a successful business plan. We have written about:

- the preliminaries, incorporating a title page, contents page and introduction
- our business, most notably its background, location and premises
- the products and services, and their features and main selling points
- our team, including ourselves, our colleagues and our employees
- the market, customers and competitors
- our objectives in the short, medium and long term

Compiling the financial section

On Tuesday, we worked through the commercial section. Now, we turn our attention to the accompanying financial section which will be included in the plan if it is to be used to raise finance, attract investment or monitor financial progress. This section might include:

- a profit budget
- a cash-flow forecast
- annual accounts
- financial requirements

A profit budget

This budget is concerned with how profitably the firm is trading (or not!) – an example of a profit-budget form is shown on page 46. The budget can be broken down into various parts and tackled accordingly:

- sales
- direct costs
- overheads
- profits
- explanatory notes
- supporting documents

Sales

We have already anticipated our sales income for the coming year and commented on it in our commercial section. We should now write out our estimated monthly sales in the budget boxes across the form. It is important that we record these sales when we expect them to be made rather than paid for as we are concentrating here on whether or not the business is making sufficient money. The timings of income and expenditure and their effects on our cash resources are looked at later when we tackle the cash-flow forecast.

Direct costs

Direct – or 'variable' – costs fluctuate directly in line with the number of goods produced and sold: the higher the level of sales, the higher the direct costs – and vice versa! There are two main categories of direct cost: 'materials' covers expenditure on raw materials, component parts, packaging and deliveries, whilst 'wages' refers to the sums paid to production-line workers, sales representatives and the like. We need to note the monthly amounts involved here in the appropriate budget columns. Deducting direct costs from sales leaves us with our 'gross profit'.

Profit-budget form

	Month:		Month:		Month:		Month:		Month:		Month:		Totals:	
	Budget	Actual	Budget	Actual	Budget	Actual	Budget	Actual	Budget	Actual	Budget	Actual	Budget	Actual
Sales														
Less: materials														
wages														
Gross profit														
Overheads: salaries														
Rent, rates, water														
Insurance														
Repairs, renewals														
Heat, light, power														
Postage														
Printing, stationery														
Transport														
Telephone														
Professional fees														
Depreciation														
Interest charges														
Other														
Total overheads														
Trading profit														

Overheads

These are those fixed items of expenditure such as rent and rates which have to be paid come what may, however many goods are being produced or sold. We need to add up the estimated annual cost of each category of overhead, divide the total by 12 and place the resulting monthly figures in the correct boxes. Remember, we are focusing here on *profit*, not cash-flow. Totting up the various entries in the monthly columns gives us our 'total overheads'. Subtracting these from our gross profit leaves us with our 'trading profit'.

Profits

Our gross and trading profit figures are very important to us. The gross profit figure shows how efficiently we are buying, manufacturing and selling goods. Our 'gross profit margin' can be calculated by dividing gross profit by sales and multiplying by 100. The resulting figure can then be compared with the trade average, and conclusions can be drawn about our performance. The trading profit figure, in turn, tells us if the business is truly profitable, and, if so, whether or not satisfactory levels of profit are being achieved.

Explanatory notes

The profit budget is only as good as its explanatory notes. After all, *we* may know why we have included certain figures, but the bank manager or whoever else is studying it might not – so we need to tell them! Thus, we should put '1', '2', '3' next to 'Sales', 'Materials', 'Wages' and so on, and attach one or two typed A4 sheets which set out each item on a point-by-point basis and explain how we arrived at our figures. We have to convince the reader that what we've put will be correct.

Here is an example of what we could write:

10 Postage

We have budgeted to spend £20 per week on general correspondence with existing and prospective customers. This is in line with last year's spending – see 'Appendix 6, Annual Accounts', pages 13–14.

11 Printing/stationery

Westbridge Printing will supply us with their standard pack of letterheads, compliment slips, business cards and envelopes at a cost of £520. Refer to 'Appendix 7, Miscellaneous Quotes', pages 15–22.

Supporting documents
Wherever possible, figures and explanatory notes must be backed up by hard, independent evidence. We need to accumulate items such as sales orders, suppliers' price lists, estimates and quotations as we go along, referring to them in our notes and including them in our accompanying appendices. Ideally, everything we mention here should be verified in the appendices by another person or organisation of some standing.

A cash-flow forecast

It is essential that a business not only makes a profit but always has enough cash reserves available to pay the bills and keep trading comfortably. A cash-flow forecast shows how money flows into and out of a firm over a given period of time. An example of a typical form is shown overleaf. The forecast can be viewed in several ways, but the following elements must be involved in its completion:

- receipts
- payments
- balances
- supplementary notes
- back-up materials

Receipts

Incomings will probably derive from three main sources: capital introduced by us, cash from sales made, and cash from debtors (those people or organisations which owe us money). We need to note the relevant amounts in the appropriate budget boxes according to when we expect the money to be *received*. We ought to be rather pessimistic here as it will often be much later than anticipated. Totting up each month's budgeted receipts enables us to complete our 'total receipts' line.

Payments

Most of the relevant information here can be lifted from our profit budget but amended to take account of the timings of outgoings – which will hopefully occur *after* incomings so that a healthy cash-flow is maintained at all times. Adding up each month's budgeted payments then allows us to write out the 'total payments' line.

Balances

If we deduct our total monthly receipts from payments, we will be left with our 'net cash-flow': and this should be a

Cash-flow forecast

	Month:		Month:		Month:		Month:		Month:		Totals:	
	Budget	Actual	Budget	Actual	Budget	Actual	Budget	Actual	Budget	Actual	Budget	Actual
Receipts: capital												
Cash from sales												
Cash from debtors												
Total receipts (A)												
Payments: creditors												
Salaries, wages												
Rent, rates, water												
Insurance												
Repairs, renewals												
Heat, light, power												
Postage												
Printing, stationery												
Transport												
Telephone												
Professional fees												
Capital payments												
Interest charges												
Other												
VAT payable												
Total payments (B)												
Net cash flow (A-B)												
Opening bank balance												
Closing bank balance												

positive rather than a negative sum if we are operating a cash-conscious firm. As relevant, we then add or subtract this amount to or from our 'opening bank balance,' which gives us our 'closing bank balance', for the month. This figure then becomes the opening bank balance for the *next* month, and so on across to the 'totals' column on the right-hand side of the form.

Supplementary notes
All too often, bank managers are sent a highly detailed forecast and are then expected to interpret it correctly without any help. Evidently, this is difficult to do, and will not put the reader in a good mood towards us. As with the profit budget, we should therefore note, '1', '2', '3' and so forth down the side of the form and explain the figures point-by-point on attached A4 sheets of paper.

Back-up materials
Similarly, we need to prove as far as possible that what we have forecasted will actually happen over the coming months. The best way of doing this is to refer to back-up materials, such as loan-agreement forms, letters from debtors and suppliers' terms of sale, and to include these in the appendices. Our own word and opinions are not enough proof: we need to substantiate these with comments and statements from other, independent people and firms.

Annual accounts

Having spent some time calculating our finances over the next year, it is a good idea to look at where we will be

financially at that time. We can do this by drawing up two
statements from the data accumulated so far:

- a profit and loss account
- a balance sheet

A profit and loss account
This financial statement summarises the sales, total costs
and profits or losses of a firm over a specific period of time,
usually one year. This statement is easy to put together
since almost all of the relevant information can be taken
from our profit budget. We must remember, however, to
deal only with *invoiced* income and expenditure here –
when the bills are *actually paid* is disregarded. As
appropriate, one or two explanatory notes may need to be
added for clarification purposes.

Here is an example of a profit and loss account:

Sales		368,327
Opening stock	42,322	
Purchases	127,400	
Closing stock	44,170	
Cost of sales		125,552
Gross profit		242,775

Overheads:

Salaries/wages	67,528	
Rent/rates/water	36,240	
Insurance	5,750	
Repairs/renewals	2,300	
Heat/light/power	1,060	
Postage	1,030	
Printing/stationery	1,260	
Transport	1,241	
Telephone	860	
Depreciation	752	
Total		118,021
Net profit		124,754

A balance sheet

Our second statement shows our firm's assets and liabilities
at a given time and indicates how its activities have been
funded. Normally, a balance sheet will be drawn up at
yearly intervals alongside of a profit and loss account.
Much of the data contained within it can be lifted from our
profit-budget and cash-flow forecast forms. An example of
a balance sheet is shown on page 55.

Fixed assets		159,600
Current assets:		
Stock	32,300	
Debtors	5,750	
Cash	5,620	
	43,670	
Current liabilities:		
Overdraft	2,600	
Creditors	9,720	
	12,320	
Net current assets		31,350
Net assets		190,950
Funded by:		
Owners' capital		45,000
Bank loan		45,000
Profit		100,950
		190,950

'Fixed assets' are those permanent items of long-term value, like land, buildings, equipment and machinery. Of greater day-to-day concern are the 'current assets', which are the ever-changing items, such as stock, debtors and cash, that come and go during trading. 'Current liabilities', like a bank overdraft and debts to suppliers, need to be settled in the near future, usually within 12 months. Subtracting current liabilities from current assets leaves us with our 'net current assets' (or 'net current liabilities' as the case may be). Adding or deducting these to or from our fixed assets produces our overall 'net assets' (or again, possibly, 'net liabilities').

Under or alongside of these figures, we need to show what the firm's activities have been 'funded by'. Here, we might incorporate items such as our own capital, bank loans and profit from our profit and loss account. The total sum should be the same as that for net assets – hence, the 'balance' in the term 'balance sheet'. Again, we might add one or two supplementary comments at the bottom of the statement, just to clarify or expand on entries, as necessary.

Financial requirements

If the business plan is being prepared for a prospective lender, this is their need-to-know information. We have to tell them exactly what it is we want from them. They will want to know about:

- the finance needed
- the repayment schedule
- the security available

The finance needed
First, we must say what it is we want – a loan or an overdraft, as examples. We also need to state the exact amount. It is a good idea to ask for a little more than we might need rather than a little less. We should allow for an

extra 10% or so to allow for a margin of error in our calculations. A lender will not be impressed if we have to go back and ask for more in a month or two's time.

We should also state what we intend to use the money for (even if we think it might be obvious from what we have said before). We might need it for a new PC, printer and other items for the website we are creating. We must remember to say when we need it. This might be before the business starts, for example.

A lender will also want to know how much we are putting in financially. Most lenders want to see some financial input from a prospective borrower as it shows their commitment to the business. If we are not committed to our business idea, we cannot expect anyone else to be! As a rule, most lenders would expect an entrepreneur to put in the same amount of money as they are asking to borrow.

The repayment schedule
We should state when we are planning to repay our borrowings. This might be over 12 months or could be as long as 60 months for many borrowings. It is sensible to err on the side of caution. Too many entrepreneurs try to impress by promising repayments within 12 months. This puts unnecessary pressure on them and can damage relations with the lender if they cannot meet such a tight schedule.

We should also show the lender how we are going to make repayments. Our promises are meaningless without those hard facts and figures. We need to refer here to our profit budget, our cash-flow forecast and our projected annual accounts. We should have a margin of error built in so that

we can still make repayments even if someone is late in
paying us.

The security available
We will almost certainly want to make repayments from
our business profits. But we need to address the worst case
scenario. How will we make repayments if everything goes
wrong? This is the question that every reputable lender will
ask. We need to be able to answer it convincingly. For
example, we need to look to make repayments from selling
assets or even re-mortgaging our home. As always, we
need to back up what we are saying. If we have equity in
our house, we need to get a valuation from estate agents
and show our most recent mortgage statement.

Summary

We have spent Wednesday looking at how to compile the
financial section of our business plan. This involved putting
in:

- a profit budget outlining sales, direct costs,
  overheads and profits, along with explanatory notes
  and supporting documents
- a cash-flow forecast detailing receipts, payments
  and balances, plus supporting notes and back-up
  materials
- annual accounts in the form of a profit and loss
  account and a balance sheet
- our financial requirements in terms of the finance
  needed, the proposed repayment schedule and the
  security available

Adding the appendices

Today, we are going to take a look at our appendices –
those all-important items which verify and enhance the
facts and figures that we put in our commercial and
financial sections. In particular, we need to think about:

- selecting the documents
- preparing the documents
- completing the appendices

Selecting the documents

When we wrote our commercial and financial sections, we
considered those documents which supported our various
comments and details. We now need to read back over
what we stated so that we can pick the right documents for
inclusion in our appendices. Let's consider again:

- our business
- products and services
- our team
- our market
- our finances

Our business
Here, we might want to have copies of annual accounts, the business transfer agent's particulars, an accountant's assessment and any positive newspaper and magazine cuttings about our firm. A map might also be put in to indicate the firm's location and surroundings. With regard to the premises, equipment, machinery and vehicles, we might enclose photographs or scale drawings (or both), the estate agent's details, copies of the freehold deeds or leasehold agreement, the solicitor's comments, a surveyor's report, and copies of planning-permission documents, sales documents and hire-purchase agreements, as relevant.

Products and services
To substantiate and enhance the data given about our goods and services, we could incorporate samples or photographs as appropriate, production schedules, suppliers' price lists, independent test results plus our own price guides, sales literature, and advertising and other promotional materials. We might then put in the same (or abbreviated) information about our rivals' products and services.

Our team

The information that we gave about our team – us, our colleagues and our employees – can be backed up by including curricula vitae, copies of certificates and diplomas, newspaper, magazine or on-line features, and copies of either the partnership-agreement or company-formation documents, as relevant. It is important to support any legal papers with a solicitor's letter explaining these. Estimates of professional fees to be incurred for work done externally rather than in-house would be useful additions too.

Our market

To back up the details provided about our customers, competitors and the marketplace, we should think about putting in a map highlighting their respective locations, along with customer sales records, orders and any research findings we have obtained about our customers. For our competitors, we could include materials similar to those used to substantiate facts and figures about our business –

press cuttings, photographs and whatever else is available and relevant. Trade-association reports about the marketplace may be helpful additions as well.

Our finances
Here, it would be a good idea to include proof of any capital available, quotes and estimates of costs and overheads, letters or other documentation from creditors and debtors confirming payment dates, and proof of security that can be put forward as and when loan facilities are provided. Not surprisingly, much of the supporting evidence we might put here will already have been included elsewhere – in customers' sales orders for example.

We have talked a lot about what we should place in our appendices – and rightly so, because they are of crucial importance. It may be beneficial at this point to look at the following master checklist, ticking off those items we intend to incorporate, and perhaps adding others, as relevant to us.

- Annual accounts
- Business transfer/estate agent's particulars
- Accountant's comments
- Newspaper/magazine cuttings and/or on-line features about the business, products, team etc.
- Photographs/drawings of premises, equipment, machinery, products etc.
- Copies of freehold deeds/leasehold agreement, plus solicitor's comments
- Surveyor's report
- Copies of planning permission

- Sales documents/hire-purchase agreements
- Product samples
- Production schedules
- Suppliers' price lists
- Independent test results
- Our price guides, sales, advertising and promotional literature
- Data on rival goods and services
- Curricula vitae
- Copies of partnership-agreement/company-formation documents, with solicitor's comments
- Customer-sales records and orders
- Customer-research findings
- Data about competitors
- Trade-association reports
- Proof of capital
- Quotes/estimates of costs and overheads
- Creditors'/debtors' letters
- Proof of security
- What else can you think of that's relevant to you?

Preparing the documents

Some of our documents may be complex and lengthy in nature, and the reader will need help to find the key information in them. To assist the reader here, let's take a look at what we can do to improve our:

- external documents
- internal documents

External documents
The external documents that we are going to put in our appendices might come from a wide variety of different sources, such as these:

• accountants	• European government
• business transfer agents	• media
• estate agents	• solicitors
• chambers of commerce	• suppliers
• colleges and universities	• surveyors
• customers	• trade bodies
• local government	• the Internet
• national government	

Wherever possible, we should try to include the original documents, unless they are especially valuable or difficult to replace. The originals are always more believable than photocopies which have sometimes been used to disguise altered documentation. Copies of the originals should be retained for our own records, though.

It is sensible to study each externally supplied item in turn – sales literature, accounts, press clippings or whatever – to decide which parts are most relevant to our text and of interest to the reader. Highlight these areas with a marker pen to focus the reader's attention on them and away from other, less relevant information.

Where necessary, be prepared to add an explanatory comment at the side or bottom of a page – a definition of a trade expression, an interpretation of a set of figures, or the date of an unmarked magazine article. We must always bear in mind who is reading our business plan and amend our text to suit them – after all, they may not know as much as we do, or indeed anything about our activities at all!

With lengthier items such as a lease or trading accounts for several years, it can be useful to attach a summary of the key facts, for easy reference purposes. This should be set out on a point-by-point basis, and be as brief and concise as possible. Hard facts, rather than opinions, should be put across: the reader can reach an opinion of their own.

Internal documents
Some of the documents that are going into the appendices will come from in-house sources or will be put together by outsiders acting upon our instructions. We might obtain such assorted documents from:

- our own books and records
- the purchasing department
- the production department
- the marketing department
- the administration department
- the finance department
- the personnel department
- photographers
- illustrators
- printers

It is advisable again to put in the originals, even if they are scruffy and perhaps completed in an idiosyncratic manner!

Obviously, a messy set of sales records is not ideal, but at least they are real and believable, and thus far better than those which look false and artificial because they have been rewritten in a new book. And again, we need to highlight key areas, and add explanatory notes and a summary of important facts, if necessary, to make the reading that much easier for our recipient.

There will be materials which we can personally compose specially for this business plan – most notably, curricula vitae, scale drawings of our premises and a summary of customer research findings. Perhaps we surveyed our customers to discover their purchasing habits and opinions. It is sensible to make sure that these documents match the overall, professional image of the rest of the plan, being attractive, easy to understand, realistic and so on. The dos and don'ts of writing a commercial and a financial section apply just as much to the appendices, whenever possible.

Remaining items that may be prepared for us upon our suggestions might include photographs or illustrations (or both) of business premises and goods, sales, advertising and promotional material, and legal documents such as partnership agreements. Evidently, we need to make it absolutely clear what we want and why, but after that we should allow ourselves to be guided by the photographer, illustrator or whomever. After all, we will be paying for their expertise, so we should certainly make the most of it!

Completing the appendices

Now that we have selected and prepared our documents, we must complete the appendices by deciding upon their:

- individual order
- overall position
- general accessibility

Individual order
It is advisable to put the documents in the same order that they were referred to in the commercial and financial sections. Thus, the reader can simply look at each in sequence, referring back to an earlier item as and when required. Avoid the temptation to bring neater and more attractive items to the front and hide other, messy documents at the back, since this will only bewilder and confuse the reader.

Overall position

If we have relatively few documents to include, our appendices can be placed after the commercial and financial sections, all together in the same file. On the other hand, should there be many lengthy or bulky items, it is better to put them in a separate file or folder. Ideally, this should be marked 'Appendices', and will match the main file in order to uphold that all-essential, professional image.

General accessibility

We must provide a list of our appendices somewhere to help the reader who wants to dip in and out as appropriate. If our appendices have been slotted in at the back of the main file, we can detail numbers, titles and pages for the various documents at the bottom of our contents page.

If, however, we have placed our appendices in a second file or folder, we could add something along the lines of, 'Our appendices are in the accompanying file' to the contents page and then affix a list of numbers, titles and pages to the front of this back-up folder. It all makes it that much easier for the reader to find their way around!

Just to add that final touch, we can attach white page-number stickers to the top right corner of each page of the appendices – 'Appendix 6: Estate Agent's Letter: Page 17', 'Appendix 6: Continued: Page 18' and so forth. This enables the reader to find the exact page they want, almost instantly.

Summary

On Thursday, we considered adding appendices to finish our business plan. This meant that we had to:

- select the right documents to support our comments about our business, products and services, team, market and finances
- prepare both external and internal documents so that they could be found and read easily
- complete the appendices by sorting out their individual order, overall position and general accessibility

Submitting a business plan

We now know how to write a business plan, but if it is to be considered a success, we need to have our proposal accepted by the prospective lender, investor or whomever. Therefore, we should focus our attention on submitting our plan properly. This means:

- writing an introductory letter
- delivering the plan
- preparing for a meeting

Writing an introductory letter

It is courteous to send an introductory letter ahead of, or with, a business plan which is going to be studied by someone from outside our organisation, such as a bank manager or would-be investor. As a first point of contact, this letter should convey an impression of smooth professionalism. If we can achieve this, the recipient may be more inclined, or even keen, to read our entire plan. Thus, we need to think carefully about the letter's:

- appearance
- contents
- style

Appearance
If the letter is sent separately in advance of a plan being delivered in person, then we need to begin by considering the envelope. A scruffy, dog-eared one with a misspelt

name or address is not going to put the reader in a favourable mood towards us. We need to choose a top-quality envelope which matches the enclosed paper, rather than a nondescript buff one. The recipient's *correct* name, job title, address and postcode should be printed carefully in the centre of the front of the envelope. A rubber stamp of our firm's name or logo, imprinted at the top left opposite the first-class stamp, adds a classy touch.

Letterheaded and watermarked A4 paper is a must if we want to be taken seriously. Similarly, a typed letter is more formal and professional in appearance than a handwritten one; the text itself has to look neat and easy to read. Generous margins to the top, sides and bottom of the page are helpful, as are short paragraphs of equal length. Tidy and error-free text is just as important: incorrectly spelt or missed-out words make us look careless and amateurish – we should always *rewrite* a letter rather than post it off with any flaws.

Contents

At the top of the page, we should have our letterhead, incorporating the firm's name, address, telephone number, fax number, e-mail address and/or web site and logo, as relevant. Next, we should type in the date of our letter, putting '17 May 2002' rather than '17th May 2002' or an abbreviation such as '17-5-02' or '17/5/02' which looks sloppy. Under this, we need to detail the reader's name, job title and address. If in *any* doubt, we should check these out – especially their sex, their initials and the precise spelling of their surname. Making a mistake here could irritate or cause offence.

Following on, we must greet the reader by name, rather than by 'Dear Sir' or 'Dear Madam' which conveys the unfortunate impression that this is no more than a circular being sent out to anybody and everyone! Below our greeting of 'Dear Mr di Carlo', 'Dear Ms Thomson' or whatever, we can indicate the subject matter of the letter by putting 'Re:' and a heading which sums up what we are writing about. We could underline this for emphasis if we wish.

Then, we come to the main part of our letter. Typically, we might say who we are and what our business is, if the recipient is likely to be unaware of these points. Moving on, we can then explain the plan itself and say why we have drawn it up and sent it (or why we are *going* to send it) to them. It can be helpful to outline what will happen next – the plan will arrive tomorrow, we will make an appointment to see them in a week's time, or whatever. We need to keep this very brief and to the point. It is an introductory letter, and no more. All of the key information is in the business plan, so we do not have to repeat anything here.

After this, we should end our letter with 'Yours sincerely' or the less formal 'Kind regards' or 'Best regards', as preferred. It is sensible to provide a clear, readable signature rather than one adorned with swirls and embellishments or a rushed and careless squiggle – neither type will impress. Finally, we should add our name and job title, if relevant. 'Enc.' or 'Enclosure' can also be put on a letter if it is being submitted with the business plan itself.

Style

As with the commercial and financial sections of our plan, the letter has to be clear and easy to understand. We must use language to suit the recipient – perhaps technical for a fellow expert, and simplified for a non-specialist. Short words, phrases and sentences tend to be unambiguous and less likely to be misinterpreted. In-house slang, local expressions and personal quirks all increase the possibility of misunderstandings.

It is worth stressing here that the letter *must* be concise. We are simply introducing ourselves and our business plan — *not* trying to give our life history or details of all the ins and outs of the plan. We should therefore check over what we have written, asking ourselves whether the points we have made are relevant to the recipient, and if they are not, we must eliminate them. Then, we need to consider whether we have set out those key points as briefly as we can, watching out for waffle or repetition.

Here is a checklist we can use when writing our letter:

- A top-quality envelope, matching the paper
- The correct name, job title, address and postcode of the recipient on the envelope
- A rubber stamp of our firm's name or logo
- A first-class stamp; it's a first-class proposal!
- Letterheaded and watermarked A4 paper
- Typed, not handwritten; we're professionals!
- Neat and easy-to-read text, using suitable language
- Tidy, error-free text, concise and to the point
- The date
- The reader's name, job title and address – correct again!
- A personal greeting – not 'Dear Sir' or 'Dear Madam'
- The subject matter, 'Re:'
- The main text – who we are, what our business is etc.
- 'Yours sincerely', or similar
- A clear, readable signature
- Our name and job title
- 'Enclosure', if appropriate

It may be useful to look at an example of a good introductory letter:

Gayther Plumbing and Heating Services
76 Thomas Road, Padbury, Sussex ME12 3BB
Tel/Fax: 01724 994312
E-mail: gayther@nvc.com

15 July 2002

Mr B Stone
The Manager
Padbury Bank plc
72 High Street
Padbury
Sussex
ME11 6BT

Dear Mr Stone

Re: 'Brightwell's'

I am a self-employed plumber who wishes to buy the 'Brightwell's' shop at 64 High Street, Padbury.

As I require some financial assistance to purchase and develop this going concern, I am writing to ask if Padbury Bank would consider helping me. A business plan detailing all relevant information is enclosed for your attention.

I have booked an appointment for 11 o'clock on 22 July so that we can discuss this matter in more detail.

I look forward to meeting you.

Yours sincerely

John Gayther

John Gayther

Enclosure

Delivering the plan

Many people spend ages putting together a first-rate business plan but then fail to deliver it properly. It needs to reach the recipient in an excellent condition in order to create that professional image we are seeking to convey. Just as important, it must arrive *on time*, especially if we are going to see the bank manager or whomever in a week or so: they have to be given sufficient time to study the material in depth, think of questions and draw conclusions before our meeting. There are three main ways of delivering our plan:

- by post
- in person
- via an intermediary

By post
Posting the business plan may be a necessity – perhaps we are trying to raise finance to start a business some distance from where we live, and are approaching a bank or building society in that area. If so, we need to make sure that it is wrapped securely – an apparently obvious point maybe, but it is not unknown for bank managers to receive plans through the post which have burst apart during transit. Not only does this put across a rather shabby image, but it could also damage the business plan itself, making it difficult to read. It is also sensible to send it by registered post so that delivery is guaranteed on a particular day, and even before a certain time. A registered delivery has an aura of importance about it too – just what we want!

Submitting our business plan by post is probably not the ideal method of delivery though – after all, once it is out of our hands, we have lost control, and something could go wrong. Even if nothing goes wrong, we will still be worrying about it for a day or so and making unnecessary (and potentially irritating) 'phone calls to check its safe arrival.

In person
Clearly, the safest way of getting our plan to the person in an excellent condition and on time is to give it to them personally. If we speak to their secretary or whomever in advance, our neat and tidy file or folders can be taken in when we know that they are free and perhaps have an hour or so available to look through our material. Making sure that we ourselves appear equally neat and presentable, we should do no more at this point than introduce ourselves, explain why we are here and hand across the plan. We should end by saying that we look forward to hearing from

them shortly or that we will make (or have made) an appointment to see them in a week's time. This may be wiser, especially if we want a reasonably prompt decision.

Of course, it is not always easy to simply say hello, hand over the business plan and then withdraw as we ought to do at this stage. We may be drawn into a conversation we are ill prepared for, or could be asked questions that we have not yet thought of or thought through. We might not put across the right image, and could even make fools of ourselves.

Via an intermediary
Perhaps it is most sensible to leave our file or folders with an intermediary such as a receptionist, the recipient's secretary or personal assistant, or another responsible member of their staff. This way, we can present it in a professional manner, and know it has arrived and *when* it is likely to be seen by that recipient. Thus, we avoid the problems of packaging, postal damage or loss, and any

potential embarrassment from a face-to-face encounter we have not prepared for fully.

Preparing for a meeting

Ideally, our business plan stands alone, containing all of the commercial and financial information and supporting materials necessary for the recipient to reach a decision – hopefully in our favour! Nevertheless, in most cases we will be expected to attend a meeting to discuss the plan and answer any questions relating to it. By arranging this meeting for a week after the plan has been delivered, we give the recipient a chance to read it, and ourselves sufficient time to prepare for this make-or-break encounter.

When preparing, we should consider three areas in particular:

- our approach
- their questions
- our answers

Our approach
We must make certain that our appearance is appropriate for the meeting. Smart dress – collar, tie and so on – is generally a sensible choice because it acknowledges the importance of the occasion, and shows our respect for the recipient of the business plan. Obviously, it does also depend largely on individual circumstances though. If we know and are on friendly terms with the person, then we can wear whatever would be considered acceptable by them – 'smart but casual', for example. At the same time,

however, we need to feel comfortable. A thick jacket, itchy new top, tight trousers and pinched shoes will feel unpleasant and distract us from the conversation.

How we speak is often regarded as being as important as our appearance. We must ensure that we are heard clearly, achieving this by holding up our head, opening our mouth wide and speaking out in a firm, strong voice. We need to sound confident, sure of our facts and enthusiastic too – if we are not, *they* won't be either. Speaking slowly to emphasise key points can be a good idea as well.

Some thought should be given to our manner during the meeting. We must avoid seeming brash and overconfident, or nervous and servile at the other extreme. Ideally, we should be friendly and sincere, and ready to answer any questions in a polite and positive way. We can help to convey this impression by looking interested throughout, leaning forward and maintaining eye contact and remaining fairly still at all times.

Their questions

Not surprisingly, our main worry when we are preparing to meet the bank manager, or whoever has received our business plan, concerns the questions we are likely to be asked. Generally, these questions fall into two broad categories: those arising from the contents of the plan and those relating to the recipient's knowledge of external factors of which we may well be unaware.

Any questions regarding what we put in the commercial and financial sections will probably be asked in order to check facts, clarify vague or confusing text or deal with any omissions. For example, we may not have mentioned a competitor that the recipient is aware of and respects. A good way of anticipating these questions is to let a trusted colleague see the plan and prepare dummy questions for us to answer. It is also sensible to read fully through the business plan just before the meeting to remind ourselves of exactly what we stated and why.

Most of the questions raised will simply seek confirmation of or further information about what we have stated: Why did we put this or that? Is this realistic? What would happen if that payment was not received on time? and so forth. We should be able to handle these comfortably if we know what we are doing, have anticipated the questions in advance and thought of our replies. Unfortunately, there may be one or two questions dealing with issues we do not know about, such as a new competitor who is to start trading soon. These are harder to predict and handle, and so we need to think about how we are going to answer any tricky questions *before* we go into that meeting.

THE PRICE OF FISH IN KATHMANDU? I HAVE NO IDEA!

Our answers

When we are asked a question during the meeting, our answer should be an honest one even if it reveals a problem or a lack of knowledge about something. The recipient will not expect this to be a perfect proposal – simply because such a proposal doesn't exist! – and may be happy to help address a difficulty or add to our understanding. They will certainly be more impressed by our honesty than by a waffly response or an obvious lie which would damage our reputation, perhaps irreparably.

If a problem becomes apparent, we should face it, outline our plans for tackling it (or at least coping with it) and then ask for the recipient's opinion. 'What do you think?' flatters the recipient, puts them in a positive mood towards us and may even produce the solution! Should we be unaware of the answer to a particular question, we should say something like, 'I'm sorry, I don't know, but I'll find out and let you know', which shows initiative. Alternatively, we could reply with, 'I'm sorry, I don't know. What information do you have?' if it seems likely that the recipient understands the situation.

Generally, everything we say during this meeting must be brief and to the point – we should adopt the attitude that the recipient's time is valuable and that we do not want to waste any of it. Our comments and responses must be easy to understand too – we should use simple words, sentences and phrases which are suited to the recipient's level of knowledge and understanding of the subject matter.

Naturally enough, what we have to say has to be realistic rather than hopeful – most bank managers have heard it all before and will be distinctly unimpressed by pipe dreams. We should refer when necessary to back-up materials in the appendices. Again, a bank manager wants hard facts, not ifs, buts and maybes.

Summary

Today, we worked on the submission of our plan, and learned how to:

- write an introductory letter with appropriate appearance, contents and style
- deliver the plan by post, in person or, preferably, via an intermediary
- prepare for a meeting by contemplating our approach and anticipating the recipient's questions and our answers

Presenting a business plan

Having submitted our business plan to the bank manager
or whomever, we can now move on to *present* it to them.
Today we will deal with:

- attending a meeting
- receiving a response
- reviewing our activities

Attending a meeting

If the meeting that we arranged a week or so ago is going
ahead, then this is a very good sign: it indicates that the
recipient has studied the plan and is in favour of it, or is at
least open to persuasion. If they were unimpressed, we
would almost certainly have heard from them by now with
a rejection letter or 'phone call.

We can view the meeting as involving three distinct stages:

- the beginning
- the middle
- the end

The beginning
Perhaps the most important piece of advice to be given
here – and it is not always followed – is to *turn up on time*.
There is nothing more likely to annoy the recipient than
being kept waiting. If they are, they may be in a rotten
mood and we will have less time to discuss our plan. It can
be a good idea to make the journey the day before to see
how long it takes to get there.

Even if we do not feel it, we should try to appear calm and
confident when we walk in, introducing ourselves to the
receptionist or whoever is going to announce our arrival to
the recipient. We must be prepared to smile, make eye
contact and shake hands with the recipient when we come

face-to-face with them. Small talk about the weather and our journey may have to be made as well.

When entering the room, we should wait to be shown to our seat rather than sitting down straight away: we may choose the wrong seat, which would be embarrassing for us. We should also decline politely any offer of a drink, sweet or cigarette. These are all potential dangers to us: we could splutter, choke or cough over them, which is distracting and even at times humiliating. It is best to sit there smiling, waiting for the bank manager to talk.

The middle
However long the meeting lasts – perhaps 15 to 30 minutes – most of the time will be taken up by the recipient working through the business plan and asking questions about the commercial section, financial section and so on. Hopefully, we will have anticipated all of the questions and can answer them succinctly, either providing an explanation, promising to find out about something, or asking the recipient what they know about a particular subject.

It is often a sensible idea to take a notebook and pen into the meeting with us. Not only does this give us something to do with our hands which we might otherwise wave about nervously, but it also makes us look professional. We can jot down useful points made by the recipient, add notes about any other work we have to do, and so forth.

Perhaps surprisingly, we should have a copy of the business plan with us too. It is not unknown for bank managers to pull apart a plan and circulate extracts of it to colleagues for their opinions. Sometimes, these are not

returned in time for our meeting. If we have full and
complete information to hand, then it all helps to make us
seem very professional and in control.

The end
Hopefully, a decision will be made towards the end of the
meeting, or an indication of the likely decision will at least
be given, subject to confirmation by the recipient's
superiors. If, however, it is not forthcoming, we should not
press for it as this can cause embarrassment or even
offence. We should simply allow the recipient to draw the
meeting to a conclusion, thank them for seeing us, smile
and leave in a pleasant and friendly manner.

After the meeting, we could send a polite letter to the
recipient thanking them again for meeting us and stating
that we look forward to hearing from them within a certain
length of time, typically one to two weeks at most. This is
courteous *and* it puts a time limit on their decision. After
all, if they are going to reject it, we want to take the plan
elsewhere, and soon!

Receiving a response

If a decision has not been announced by the close of our
meeting – perhaps because the business plan has to be
forwarded to someone else for approval – we would expect
to receive either a formal, written response or a more
informal 'phone call from the recipient within the following
week or so. We then need to deal with the consequences of
one of the following:

- rejection
- acceptance

Rejection

A plan which is turned down and returned to us by a
potential source of finance, investment or assistance should
not just be delivered automatically to the next name and
address on our list of prospective lenders or whomever, for
clearly there may be something wrong with it. We should
try to discover *why* it was rejected by studying the letter of
rejection. Or we can 'phone the recipient for an explanation,
if that would be considered acceptable – in most instances,
it will be: after all, we should be entitled to a few minutes'
explanation after all the time and effort we have put into
our plan. However, to obtain a full and honest explanation,
we must maintain our professionalism and not attempt to
persuade them to change their mind. Their decision has
been made, and that's that!

It may be that they think the proposition is not a viable one
or at least is not for them. In either case, we should take
note of their comments, sit down and review carefully our
whole plan and its future prospects. At best, we will
probably need to make some changes and improvements to
it. At worst, it may be best not to proceed at all. Only we
can decide what to do.

Hopefully, we will decide to continue and send the revised business plan elsewhere – to a lender who has a better knowledge of our market, or an investor who is also prepared to become involved in the day-to-day running of the firm, or whomever. Prior to resubmitting it, however, we should replace any pages which have become torn or grubby, remove references included for the last recipient's benefit, and amend outdated text, facts and figures. We need to convince the new recipient that the plan has been written especially for them, and that they are the first person to receive it!

Acceptance

At some stage, and perhaps even the first time around, our proposal will be accepted and we will be offered a loan from a bank, capital from a partner or a leasehold agreement from a landlord. We can now celebrate, albeit briefly, before getting down to business again to expand, diversify, or whatever, and go on to greater success in the future.

Reviewing our activities

We are now going to look back over the week and review
our activities day by day. Let's just remind ourselves what
we studied each day:

• Sunday	Understanding business plans
• Monday	Making preparatory notes
• Tuesday	Composing the commercial section
• Wednesday	Compiling the financial section
• Thursday	Adding the appendices
• Friday	Submitting a business plan
• Saturday	Presenting a business plan

Sunday

On Sunday, we found out all we needed to know about
business plans:

- They usually contain commercial and financial sections,
  and are supported by appendices which verify and
  enhance these

- They can be used to raise finance, attract investment, encourage assistance and improve performance
- A successful business plan is well researched, adapted, attractive, understandable, realistic and backed up by independent evidence

Monday

During Monday, we made some preparatory notes by conducting internal research, using external sources and accumulating appropriate information. This meant:

- drawing on our own extensive knowledge
- talking to our colleagues in other departments
- referring to company books and records
- contacting outside individuals and organisations like banks, accountants, solicitors and the media
- approaching other external bodies as diverse as architects, photographers and market research companies
- jotting down notes under the headings 'The business', 'Products and services', 'The team', 'The market', 'Objectives', 'Finance' and 'Appendices'

Tuesday

This was the day that we composed the commercial section of the plan. We included various ingredients:

- the preliminaries – title page, contents page, introduction
- our business – background, location, premises
- products and services – features, selling points
- our team – ourselves, colleagues, employees
- the market – customers, competitors
- our objectives – short, medium and long term

Wednesday

On Wednesday, we compiled the financial section of our business plan. We incorporated:

- a profit budget outlining sales, direct costs, overheads and profits, along with explanatory notes and supporting documents.
- a cash-flow forecast detailing receipts, payments and balances, with supplementary notes and back-up materials
- annual accounts in the form of a profit and loss account and a balance sheet
- our financial requirements, and in particular the finance needed, the repayment schedule and the security available

Thursday

During Thursday, we added appendices to our commercial and financial sections. We selected and prepared documents before completing these appendices. This involved:

- picking the right documents to substantiate the information given about our business, products and services, team, market and finances
- tidying up external documents to make them easier to look at
- producing internal documents which were understandable and simple to study
- putting the documents in the right order and position, and making them accessible

Friday

This was the day that we dealt with submitting a business plan to a recipient. We considered:

- writing an introductory letter, paying special attention to its appearance, contents and style
- delivering the plan, either by post, in person or via an intermediary
- preparing for a meeting with the recipient, with particular emphasis on our approach, their questions and our answers

Saturday

Today, we have had our busiest day. We have looked at how to present a business plan to the recipient, and have contemplated:

- attending a meeting, viewing this in terms of its beginning, middle and end
- receiving a response, discussing how to respond to a rejection or acceptance of our proposal
- all our activities to date, reviewing these on a step-by-step basis

Conclusion

Writing a business plan is a key skill, and to acquire it in a week is a considerable achievement. It is important, however, that we keep working at it, learning from our errors and building on our successes, continually comparing our budgeted with our actual performance, so that we can make constant, ongoing use of this essential business tool, amending and developing it as and when necessary. If – or when – we do this, our organisation will benefit greatly as a result, whether we are using the plan to raise finance, attract investment, encourage assistance or improve performance.

SUN

MON

TUE

WED

THU

FRI

SAT

For information

on other

IN A **WEEK** titles

go to

www.inaweek.co.uk